A CHILD'S DAY
IN A CHINESE CITY

To my dear parents, So Hing Bun and Ho Sook Chun; my lovely wife, Mabel;
and my children, Ivy and Derek

Benchmark Books
Marshall Cavendish
99 White Plains Road
Tarrytown, New York 10591
Website:www.marshallcavendish.com

Library of Congress Cataloging-in-Publication Data

So, Sungwan.
In a Chinese City / by Sungwan So
p. cm. – (A childs day)
ISBN 0-7614-1224-7
1. China—Social life and customs—Juvenile literature. [1. China—Social life and customs.] I. Title. II. Series.
DS721 .S667 2001   951.009732dc21   00-069674

Designed by Sophie Pelham

Printed in Singapore

1 3 5 7 9 8 6 4 2

The Publishers would like to acknowledge Mabel Leung as cowriter of the text.

AUTHOR ACKNOWLEDGMENTS
With grateful thanks to Yikang and her family, Dr. Chiao Chien, my friends in Hong Kong and China, all the staff at Yikang's elementary school,
Shanxi Changzhi Jiandong Xiaoxue, and Lianyi Song at SOAS in London for checking the text.

A CHILD'S DAY
IN A CHINESE CITY

Sungwan So

BENCHMARK BOOKS

MARSHALL CAVENDISH
NEW YORK

AUTHOR'S NOTE

Yikang and her parents live in the city of Changzhi in the Shanxi Province of northern China. Like most other cities in China, Changzhi is a mixture of old and new: brand-new office buildings have risen right next to buildings that have been standing for hundreds of years. Yikang's home is in a suburb of the city. It's usually very quiet in this area, especially after about seven o'clock in the evening. Most people like to stay at home after work and spend time with their families.

There used to be so many Chinese people in China that people worried there wouldn't be enough room for everyone in the future. To help keep the population down, the government introduced a one-child-per-family rule. Yikang does not have any brothers or sisters, but she has plenty of friends to play with instead. Besides her classmates, she likes visiting her *biaomei* (cousin), who lives just a short walk away from Yikang's apartment building.

CHINA

Shanxi

Ren Yikang is seven years old.

She lives with her parents in a five-story apartment building in Changzhi. The apartment is provided by the local middle school where Yikang's mother, Han Xiaofang, is a teacher. Yikang's father, Ren Xuzhong, is employed by the Chinese government. His job is to help make life better for handicapped people.

REN YIKANG Ren is Yikang's family name (her surname). In China people always put their family name first and their personal name second. Yikang means "happy" and "healthy" in Chinese.

School starts at eight, so Yikang's mother wakes her up at about seven. First Yikang helps her mother make the bed, and then she goes to the bathroom to brush her teeth and wash her face.

Yikang likes milk and crackers for her breakfast, but her parents prefer traditional Chinese food. Yikang's mother is having *mantou* (steamed buns) and *chayedan* (boiled eggs soaked in tea). She even manages to persuade Yikang to have an egg too!

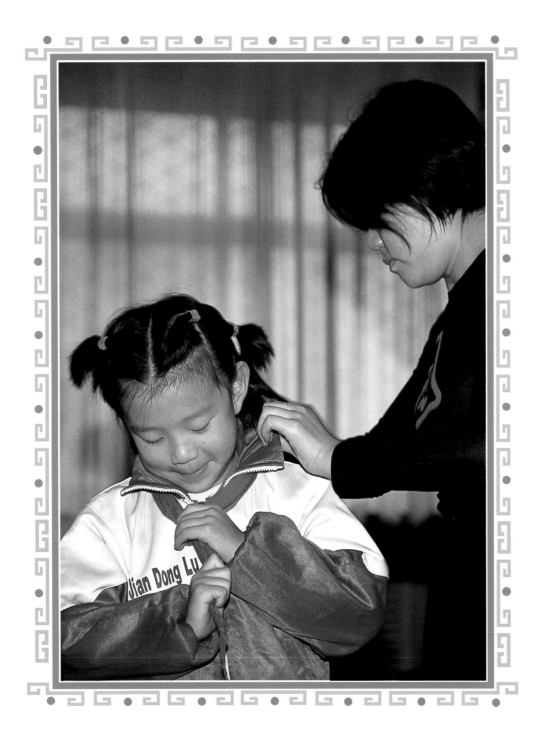

Yikang has to wear her school uniform today because there is going to be a special ceremony at school. As a member of the *Shaoxiandui* (Young Pioneers), she also has to wear a red scarf.

SHAOXIANDUI is a popular elementary school club in China, similar to the Girl Scouts and Boy Scouts.

Yikang's father gives her a lift to school on the back of his *zixingche*
(bicycle). Just like all her friends, Yikang is a big fan of the latest
American and Japanese cartoons, and her backpack is decorated with
pictures of her favorite characters.

Yikang is on school-cleaning duty this morning. She and some of her classmates mop the floors of the classrooms and the corridors outside.

It's the last school day before *Guoqingjie* (National Day), so there is a flag-raising ceremony before lessons.

GUOQINGJIE is thought of as the birthday of new China. It has been celebrated every year on October 1 since China became the People's Republic of China on October 1, 1949.

All the pupils in the school assemble in the playground and salute the Chinese flag.

Yikang's first lesson is Chinese. Today the teacher is showing them some new Chinese *wenzi* (words).

The wenzi at the top of the blackboard mean "Study hard, be inquisitive, enjoy learning, and think hard."

When the teacher asks Yikang a question, she has to stand up before giving her answer.

During recess, Yikang and her friends play kick the *jian* (shuttle-cock) outside.

13

The second lesson is arithmetic. The teacher has brought in a big *suanpan* (abacus) to demonstrate *zhusuan* (doing sums using an abacus). All the children practice at the same time using their own suanpans at their desks.

SUANPANS are calculating frames. Each bead within the suanpan frame represents a number.

After arithmetic, it's exercise time. Everyone lines up behind their class captain and listens to the instructions on the loudspeakers. They start with *yanbaojiancao* (eye exercises) to improve their eyesight.

The class captains leading the exercises make sure that everyone is completely warmed up.

15

Yikang's mother picks her up at noon, and they go to the local market.
They buy some Chinese celery and *doufu* (bean curd) for lunch.

Yikang's mother also wants to buy some ready-made frozen *shuijiao* (dumplings), so they go to the grocery store.

On their way back home, Yikang meets some of her friends. One of them is eating sunflower seeds straight from the flower.

Back at home, Yikang helps her mother prepare lunch.

Yikang's mother cooks the frozen dumplings in the *wok* (a kind of Chinese frying pan) and serves them with some vinegar and garlic. Yikang's father usually comes back for lunch, but today he phones home to say that he is too busy at work.

After lunch Yikang plays on her father's computer. She likes pretending to search for on-line information about the stock market just like he does.

Although she can play on his computer, Yikang is not allowed to touch her father's statue of *Caishen*, the Chinese god of fortune. Yikang's parents light sticks of incense in front of the statue twice a month and pray that their investments will do well.

There are many gods, great and small, in the Chinese religion. One of the most popular is Zaoshen, *the Chinese god of the stove.*

19

Yikang has to be back at school by three o'clock for afternoon lessons. Yikang and her mother's journey back takes them past some corn and *xiaomi* (millet) fields, the two most important crops grown in the area. It's harvesttime, so the farmers are busy in the fields with their tractors.

On the way, Yikang's mother stops to have the tire on her bike checked.

These men are playing *xiangqi* (Chinese chess) to pass the time while their bikes are being repaired.

The first lesson of the afternoon is *meishu* (art). Today the teacher wants the class to think about how the human body works. He programs an image into the computer so that everyone can copy it. Then he uses a video camera to film the children moving and they compare their drawings with the video.

The last lesson of the day is music. The teacher accompanies the class on the piano while they sing *"Xiaoyu Yaoxialai,"* "Rain Is Going to Fall."

At half past five, it's time to go home. For dinner tonight Yikang's mother is preparing rice and stir-fried Chinese celery with *doufu* (bean curd), sweet and sour eggplant, and sliced pig livers stewed in a thick sauce.

Sometimes Yikang's father helps with dinner, but tonight Yikang insists he play *tiaoqi* (Chinese checkers) with her.

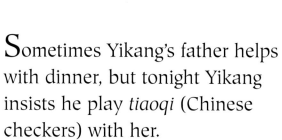

TIAOQI Each tiaoqi player has ten marbles, and the aim of the game is to move them to the opposite corner before your opponent does. You move your marbles by jumping over the other ones on the board.

24

After dinner Yikang starts her homework. Her mother is very patient and always explains things when Yikang gets stuck.

But it is difficult to concentrate on homework when the Olympic Games are about to start. Yikang and her parents want to find out if China has won any more gold medals.

26

At about ten, Yikang kisses her father good night and goes to bed. Her mother gets in with her for a while, and they read comic books until Yikang feels sleepy. *Yikang, wan'an* (Good night, Yikang).

MORE ABOUT CHINA

CHINA, THE PAST

China has a rich and ancient past that dates back thousands of years, to before even the ancient Greeks and Romans. Many of the beliefs and customs from this faraway time still live on today, so Chinese people have a great sense of history.

When tourists come to China, they often plan to visit the Great Wall in the north. The Great Wall was the idea of the very first Chinese emperor, Qinshihuang, who thought a wall would be a good way to protect China from attack. It is called "Great" because it eventually ended up being four thousand miles long and it can be seen by astronauts in space!

For most of the country's long history, the Chinese people were ruled by powerful emperors. However, this system came to an end about a hundred years ago.

In 1911 the Chinese people decided that China should belong to the people rather than to just one emperor, and they had a revolution. The People's Republic of China was formed on October 1, 1949, and the Chinese people refer to this date as the birthday of new China.

CHINA, THE LAND

China is the third largest country in the world. It has vast deserts, great mountain ranges, a huge rugged plateau in its center, and even a subtropical forest on Hainan Island in the South China Sea. It also has two great rivers: the Yellow River and the Yangtze River. The land around these two rivers is excellent for farming, so Chinese people have always settled in these areas. However, it can also be very dangerous as the rivers often flood. Because the rivers are good in some ways and bad in others,

Chinese people think of them as untamed dragons. When the rivers are happy, they bring prosperity, but when they are angry, they bring disasters.

RELIGION IN CHINA

Many people in China are Buddhists or Taoists. Some are Christians and Muslims, but by far the most popular religious practice in China is ancestor worship. Most Chinese people believe that all the important people in China's history, and all their family members who lived before them, still play an important part in family life. They often set up small shrines in their homes in honor of these ancestors. They burn sticks of incense at the shrines and sometimes serve their ancestors fruits, wine, or tea. (Of course, the ancestors can't really eat or drink these gifts, but they are offered to them as a sign of respect.) If it's one of the ancestor's birthdays or the anniversary of one of their deaths, people usually burn paper money and offer chicken or pork to their ancestor to mark the occasion.

CHINA, THE PEOPLE

China has the world's largest population—about 1,270,000,000 people—and millions of other Chinese people live all over the world outside China.

In ancient times, most people in China worked on the land and depended on the changing of seasons for their livelihood. To help people plan, a special Chinese calendar was developed that divided the year into twenty-four climatic sections, or *jieqi*. China is no longer just a farming country, but rural people still like to do things according to the season. Couples often get married in winter, for example, because this isn't such a busy time for farming.

LANGUAGE IN CHINA

China is a very big country and it has many different regions. Each region has its own way of speaking, and although today the official language of China is Mandarin, Chinese people still speak to each other in their own dialect (or local language) when they go about their daily lives.

Before Mandarin was introduced about a hundred years ago, it was difficult for people from different parts of China to talk to each other, and they relied on the Chinese writing system to communicate—even if they didn't share the same spoken language, they all had the same way of writing. Chinese writing is very different from English (which is based on sounds), because it is based on picture symbols called characters. When the first Chinese characters were invented more than three thousand years ago, each character looked like a picture of what it meant. For example, the character meaning *claw* looked like a bird's footprint, the character meaning *moon* looked like a crescent moon, and the character meaning *horse* looked like a running horse.

Written Chinese has developed a lot since then, and Chinese people today use as many as five thousand different characters just for everyday writing. Other Asian languages, such as Japanese and Korean, use characters based on the Chinese system for their writing too.

SOME CHINESE WORDS AND PHRASES

zao'an (zow-an)—good morning

Ni hao ma? (nee how ma)—How are you?

xiexie (shair-shair)—thank you

Wo de mingzi jiao Yikang (wer der ming-ze gee-ow Yikang)—My name is Yikang.

Duoduo baozhong! (dur-dur bow-chong)—Look after yourself!

THE CHINESE WORDS IN THE BOOK

biaomei—cousin

Caishen—the Chinese god of fortune

Changzhi—the city in Shanxi Province where
Yikang lives

chayedan—boiled eggs soaked in tea with
seasonings

doufu—bean curd, made from soy bean milk
(sometimes called "tofu")

Guoqingjie—National Day in China, celebrated
on October 1

jian—shuttlecock

jieqi—the seasons in the Chinese year

Mandarin—the official language of China

mantou—steamed buns

meishu—art

Qinshihuang—the first Chinese emperor

Shaoxiandui—Young Pioneers, a popular
elementary school club

shuijiao—dumplings

suanpan—abacus, a counting device with
beads, used to do sums

tiaoqi—Chinese checkers

wenzi—Chinese characters or words

wok—a Chinese cooking pan with steep sides
and a rounded bottom

xiangqi—Chinese chess

xiaomi—millet, a cereal crop grown in the
fields near Yikang's apartment

"Xiaoyu Yaoxialai"—the title of a song: "Rain Is
Going to Fall"

yanbaojiancao—eye exercises

Yangtze River—the longest river in China

Yellow River—the second longest river in China

Yikang, wan'an—Good night, Yikang

Zaoshen—the Chinese god of the stove

zhusuan—doing sums using an abacus

zixingche—bicycle

FIND OUT MORE

Dawson, Zoe. *China.* Austin, Texas: Raintree Steck-Vaughn, 1995.

Flint, David. *China.* Austin, Texas: Raintree Steck-Vaughn, 1993.

King, David C. *China.* Vero Beach, Florida: Rourke Book Co., 1995.

INDEX

arithmetic lessons 14

art lesson 22

bedtime 27

bicycles 9, 21

breakfast 7

cartoons 9

Chinese checkers 24

Chinese chess 21

Chinese flag 11

cleaning duty 10

dinner 24

exercise 15

games 13, 21, 24

geography 28–29

Great Wall of China 28

history 11, 28–29, 30

homework 25

language 12, 30–31

lunch 18

music lesson 23

names 5

National Day 11

religion in China 19, 29

rivers 28–29

school 10–15, 22–23

school uniform 8

shopping 16–17

television 26

washing 6